To / ~~Gucci~~

# A ~~mazi~~ng

# *Angels*

Mush love ♡

Louise x

Copyright © 2023
All rights reserved. This book or any portion thereof may not be reproduced or used in any manner whatsoever without the express written permission of the author.

ENTER ISBN HERE 9798378006977

# *Activating Angels*

## *Easy and Effortless Connection for Your Everyday Life*

By Louise Green

# Welcome to the Magic

## Introduction Part One

# This is Me

Welcome.

Thank you for taking a leap of faith and opening this book. It is an honour to be able to bring this to you. This is not like anything you will have read or heard before.

I am Louise, and I am 53 years old. I am a Wife, a Mother, a Grandmother and a Pug Mum.

I have the same day to day expectations put upon me as most other women. I have a job; I take care of my home and love and support my family to the best of my ability. I face those same life challenges that crop up like the car breaking down, the washing machine going bang, or putting your back out whilst tying your shoelaces and having to cancel your plans.

*I also have a team of Angels that I talk to every day who guide and support me in all areas of my life.*

So, why have I written this book? Quite simply, it was given to me to understand and share with the world. There are countless wonderful books out there that can 'teach' you about Angels. You can discover their names, their unique gifts, and all manner of wonderful insight into these magical beings of love and light, and all of them have their place in the world.

However, this is not one of those. This book is different. It does not cover any of that, because frankly I am just not all that interested. Yep, you read that right.

You see, I like to keep things simple, and I trust that if I *need* to know which Angel is helping me in any given moment, they will show me or tell me.

My study of the Angels is much more practical and in the moment. I have concentrated on connection, asking, and receiving guidance and that, essentially, is what this book is all about and how you can do it for yourself.

I am talking to you if you desire change in your life but can see no way how to even begin. If you have always 'known' somewhere deep inside you, that there was more to life. If you want clear, simple to understand information that you can start implementing right now, then please keep reading.

I am not here to waste your time, so expect real talk, short, to the point dialogue and absolutely no *fluff*.

This book has been 5 years in the making and is a culmination of all that I have learned to be true for me. All the soul searching, blind faith and hope that things could get better. Questioning everything and every area of my life and desiring complete change, despite having no idea how that was going to happen.

This is the story of my self-discovery and quite possibly, the beginning of yours.

### Introduction Part Two

# Let's Get Ready to Rumble

What can you expect from me, the Angels, and this book?

Real talk. Why? Because I know that your time is precious and reading this book is a gift to yourself and I want to make it easy and straightforward so you can implement these ideas as soon as possible and bring about the change you desire for your life. But remember, just because my words may challenge you, it does not mean they do not come from a place of love. You have waited long enough for change, so let us just get on with it.

I will be sharing ways to connect with your Angels and my personal experiences.

I will be sharing ideas of what Angels can help you with in your day-to-day life to get you started and used to asking for their help.

One thing that is important to remember though, is that my experiences are unique to me, and your Angels may appear in a completely different way. They may look different, sound different or show themselves in other forms such as balls of light. Whatever that looks like for you is right for you. You cannot get it wrong. Yes, you can overthink, doubt yourself and the Angels, but none of that matters. What matters is that you begin. What matters is that you try it for yourself. In a nutshell, there are no hard and harsh rules that you need to follow. I have told you I like things simple, but sometimes we like to make things more difficult than they need to be (more on this later). I am not here to tell you what you SHOULD or SHOULD NOT do. That is not my job.

I am purely a messenger. This entire book has been channelled through me by my Angels. They want you to know that that they are waiting to connect with you, and it is so much easier than you may think and so very possible for everyone. You can have a life you have always dreamed of, (whatever that looks like for you). Or you can 'just' allow them in to help you with your day-to-day life. You get to choose.

But please know this; -

*It is no coincidence that you are reading this book.*

You are here for a reason. This is meant for you. Your curiosity brought you here.

*Your Angels brought you here!*

So, just be open to the possibility that your life could be about to change forever.

We are so
glad you
are here

# One Girl and Her Angels

*One girl met her Angels*
*Whilst tucked up in her bed*
*A golden light filled up the room*
*And sparkled round her head*

*She knew that they were coming*
*For they had told her so*
*She had so many questions*
*So much she longed to know*

*They told her that they loved her*
*And that they always would*
*For she was meant to do great things*
*To be a force for good*

*Of course, the girl knew all of this*
*Despite her tender age*
*She knew her magic deep inside*
*The world would be her stage*

*When can I start doing this?*
*She asked them straight away*
*My Darling, you are doing it*
*Each and every day*

*You are a light of love and hope*
*In everything you do*
*And you inspire those around you*

*To share all their love too*

*You will make an impact*
*More than you could know*
*You will change the lives of thousands*
*And teach them how to grow*

*And they in turn will spread your word*
*To those who need to hear*
*Now you see what you must do*
*So go ahead, my dear*

*Do what you were born to do*
*For all of Humankind*
*And spread the word of love and light*
*to anyone you find*

*Now go to sleep, my Darling*
*For we have just begun*
*This journey that is called your life*
*God Bless You, Precious One*

I wrote this poem, sitting in my garden on a sunny May afternoon in 2020. The country was in chaos and full of fear due to the events that were taking place all around the world. I was re-connecting with my Angels, and they gave me this poem – the words just flowed out of me and onto the paper. I later went on to discover that the girl in the poem was me and it was a *memory*. I was starting to wake up. I was starting to *remember.*

You see, we all have Angels around us – whether you choose to believe it or not. They have been with us for lifetimes and just want to help. Am I oversimplifying them? No, I don't think so.

*Yes, they are powerful, magical, multidimensional beings, but so am I and so are you.*

Doesn't it make sense, then to collaborate? Imagine the potential, imagine the possibilities if we worked together! You are more powerful than you know, and the Angels can help you uncover that and show you what is possible for you – in the moment, in the next 24 hours or in your lifetime. They *literally* just want to help you in any way that you will allow.

So, are you joining us?

# Chapters

1. Gold
2. You'll Never Walk Alone
3. Everybody Wants to Rule the World
4. I Feel Good
5. Dear Darling

Story Time – The Hearing Aid

6. Rolling in the Deep
7. You're the Voice

Story Time – The Text Message

8. Sign of the Times

Story Time – The Car

9. Let it Go

10. How will I Know

Story Time – The Hotel Room

11. All I Ask

12. Fighter

13. No Matter What

Story Time – The Missing Cards

14. Living on a Prayer

15. Lean on Me

# Chapter One

# Gold
**(Orbs)**

Lockdown 2020, Easter Bank Holiday weekend. I am out for my hour of exercise on the beach which is close to where I live. It would usually be packed with families that have come to stay at the nearby holiday park. As I look across the expanse of beach in both directions, I cannot see another living soul (plenty of non-living) and I smile to myself. I can have a real good chat with the Angels here without any interruption.

Of course, it hadn't always been this way. For most of my adult life I had been a very angry, stressed-out human that was full of reasons why her life was so difficult and a fully-fledged victim of every circumstance.

It feels odd to write those words about myself as I haven't felt that way for so many years.

I didn't think I could or would ever find peace. I thought life was supposed to be hard and I wore the day-to-day struggle like a badge of honour. I honestly believed that was how life was supposed to be. I thought it was normal to feel burnt out, exhausted, stressed, and angry at the entire world. I worked so hard and then harder still, but it was just never enough.

I was never satisfied or felt proud of myself. I was on a giant hamster wheel of misery and the more I pushed, the harder I tried, the more it became a self-fulfilling prophecy and reflected more of the same back into my life.

Does this sound at all familiar? I *know* that there are so many of you out there that face a similar struggle. Let me tell you why.

That version of 'life' that we have been living is what we thought we were supposed to do because that is what our parents and Grandparents did before us.

They only knew hardship and sacrifice and they passed the torch down to us. We held it high in the sky like a beacon to signify the beginning of our never-ending battle with time, fear, stress, money, relationships, jobs, never feeling good enough and ultimately total exhaustion...

Well, I am going to let you in on a little secret...

**IT DOESN'T HAVE TO BE THAT WAY!**

It can be easy. It can be peaceful and calm. It can be effortless and magical. Of course, life will continue to challenge us at times because we are living in a physical world having a human experience AND THAT IS WHY WE HAVE ANGELS TO HELP US

Can I get an Amen?

    Ok, I am going to step down from my soap box for a minute because I realise that was a lot – but like I told you - I am purely channelling these words and they are FLOWING like a river right now.

    Let's back up. There was a moment in my life that put me (back) onto this path. In 2017 I became a Grandmother and when I saw my Granddaughter being born, I knew that I wanted change. Change for myself, change for her, and change for the world. Suddenly my priorities were so insignificant. I no longer cared about work because I wanted to spend time with her, creating memories and having fun. I also realised that the person that I had been up until then had a lot of work to do.

    ***And that is when the ORBS came.*** (They had always been there, but I wasn't in the right vibrational place to see them).

Every time I walked to the beach, I noticed faint gold twinkly lights around me or in the sky and it always felt good even though I didn't actually *know* it was Angels, I just knew it was something magical that was meant for me. It gave me comfort. As time progressed, I saw more and more, fluttering, silvery shimmering wings and moving coloured shapes of energy dancing across my walls and ceilings.

And, yes, I have seen an actual full-sized Angel on several occasions – each one so stunningly beautiful that all I could do was watch with complete awe and wonder at what I was seeing. There really is no way to even begin to describe them, particularly as they appear differently to each of us. It is magical and I am not talking about the Disney kind of magic, I am talking about the most powerfully bright light that is filled with nothing but unconditional love that radiates across the Universe that just happens to show up in your front room. (They are nodding in approval at my description).

So, the orbs were the beginning because once I completely trusted that there was more to life than our 3D reality and that magic really did exist, things started happening for me. People or courses would pop up on my social media. I would hear words from a song in my head, urging me to do something or go somewhere.

I started to find other like-minded women in the online space and teachers that hosted webinars and masterclasses on all this powerful stuff. I discovered a whole new world, and I just soaked it all up. I was so eager to learn about all of it. I loved to listen to people talk about Angels all day long. I threw myself into a spiritual way of life and finally felt like I was home and for the first time in years I felt *alive*. And that was just the beginning.

## Chapter Two

# You'll Never Walk Alone

One of the biggest obstacles we face when embracing our spiritual side is *unlearning* and letting go of the past. My return to spirituality started at 47 – that is almost 5 decades of old programming and limiting beliefs to deal with and face up to.

All the past traumas, hurts, memories, every time you made a mistake, embarrassed yourself, got cheated on, lost an argument, fell over in public... the list is endless. ALL of this had been replaying over and over in my mind to reaffirm what a terrible human being I was and how completely sh*t my life had been up until now and if I wanted change of any sort, I was going to have to start facing it.

I am going to be completely honest here, this realisation very nearly had me running back to my old life. It seemed like such an overwhelming task. How was I going to do that? Where do I even start with the process?

Cue the aforementioned mentors, teachers and coaches that had already been through this and were lining up to help me.

I went on a (sometimes brutal) journey of self-discovery to question everything that I thought I knew to be true and to learn to connect to my true inner self and the Angels were with me every step of the way. When I was going through something tough from my past, the Angels would tell me to go for a walk – and as I was eager to do anything other than what I was doing, I hastily made my way down to the beach.

As I walked along, I was aware of some colours hovering either side of me. I slowed down and every step I took was matched with a purple glittery footstep on one side of me and a gold footstep on the other.

"We are walking right beside you," they said. I felt so loved in that moment and it gave me so much comfort to know that I was not alone. This has happened numerous times since and it ever fails to give me goosebumps.

Looking back, I don't know if I would have got to this place without the constant reassurance, guidance, and unconditional love that I felt.

I was no longer alone. The truth is none of us are alone and although, right now, you may not feel any sort of connection, the Angels *are* with you. As we get further into it, you will be able to feel their presence and begin your own dialogue. That is my intention for every one of you that is reading this – to empower you to find your voice so you can do this for yourself.

# Angels,
# Please can today
# be easy and full of
# laughter ✨

Thank you. Thank you.
Thank you 🙏

    This is a simple, quick, and easy request that I personally use a lot – if I have a challenging workday ahead, or a difficult situation to deal with. It always lightens the mood and there is always an unexpected element that shows up – either in the form of a person that contributes to the fun or an outcome I could never have predicted.

The three Thank you's are something I learned early on, from a book called the Magic, by Rhonda Byrne and it is a practice that I adopted immediately and continue to use daily. Gratitude and giving thanks are so important and we will get into that more. I just wanted to give you an idea of what you can expect in terms of what I say and what I ask for. Right now, that might seem too much of a stretch but keep an open mind and keep going.

## Chapter Three

# Everybody Wants to Rule the World (Aka The Rules)

I am feeling that you are now all wanting some more instructions and rules to follow and that is completely understandable because that is what we have grown up to expect – to be told what we can and cannot do. To be shown the boundaries that we may not cross and the box that we must stay confined in. You have questions that you want answered, you want to know the how and the when and manage the outcome and what parameters you are permitted to work with in. So, I'm not sure if you are ready to hear this, but...

THERE. ARE. NO. RULES.

Bear with me whilst I explain why. This is about YOU – the gorgeous, perfect soul that you are. Your uniqueness is your key – it is your own personal navigation system on what works for you.

What the fudge does that mean, Louise?

It means, my Loves, that if something feels good to you, keep doing it. If it doesn't, then stop.

We all have different likes and dislikes and that is how it is supposed to be so, it makes sense, then, that when we are learning anything new that we learn in different ways. So, you may try something, and it doesn't feel good or easy. It may feel *unfamiliar* if you have never tried any kind of spiritual practice before and that is to be expected. But I am talking more about if you find yourself putting it off or avoiding doing it altogether. (Otherwise known as having the 'ick'). If that is how you are feeling, it is not for you, so move on and try something else. You haven't done anything wrong. It simply is not aligned to you and there are (thankfully), plenty of other options out there for you to try. Bear this in mind as you begin this exciting journey. There is no forcing. There is no 'should' in spiritual learning and connection. Remember this is not learning in the traditional sense. I will expand on what I mean as we get further into the book. For now, just keep in mind three things.

- ❖ Keep it simple.

- ❖ Focus on doing things that make you feel good.

- ❖ Always show gratitude - for what you have now and for your Angels, even if you are not yet convinced that they are around you.

# The Angels Angle

## Message incoming.....

There will be points where the Angels will step in with a direct message for you. It may be in the form of an Angel Card that I have been guided to pull or words that are coming through so strongly that I have had to interrupt the book and share it with you.

"We are so excited for you. This is what we have been waiting for. Now is the time for you. We cannot wait to be part of the gang and help you however you want us to.

There is nothing to fear. There is only love here and we want to share it with you!

We can already feel your connection to us as you are a truly powerful soul. Trust that this is working for you right now. Pay close attention to your surroundings for we are always with you."

I am going to give you all that you need, but it is important that you also understand why you need to do it. You must build a solid foundation and that can take time. I am five years into this now, and whilst it needn't be anywhere near this long for you *because this book will move you forward quickly and easily,* I know that some of you go-getters will jump right in regardless and I would urge you just to hang on for another couple of chapters. I also know that there are many of you sceptical souls that need more from me (us), (because we are all different, right?) So, let's just keep going for a bit longer before we get to the juicy stuff that you all came here for.

I can feel your collective frustration, right now

Just keep reading ➡️ ▢ ➡️ ▢ ➡️ ▢

Before we go any further, I want us to take a moment and *set an **intention**.*

What the fudge does that mean?

It means that we decide right here and now that we are going to wholeheartedly embrace this process. We are going to do 'the work' that is required of us. We are going to trust that this is possible for us. We are going to be open to possibilities and become more consciously aware of our surroundings.

To truly shift to a place of surrender and allowing, I really want you to close your eyes and take some nice, cleansing deep breaths whilst you let those words in. You can choose your own words and intentions if you prefer as long as it feels good to you to say it, It does not have to be a big deal, just in the moment, say to yourself what intentions you want to set and what outcome you want from doing this work.

.  It can take one minute, 5 minutes or longer, if you feel that you want to stay in that place. Always finish with whatever form of gratitude feels natural (thank you, thank you, thank you, is my gratitude of choice, but it does not have to be yours) Once again, you cannot get this wrong.

Do what feels good. Say it with conviction and belief.  You can have just one intention of simply reading the whole book before deciding if it is for you or not.  You can set many intentions, as long as they do not overwhelm you. Do not try to manage or control the outcome. Do not put specific time frames or unrealistic expectations on yourself.  Remember, we are loving ourselves and our journey is unique to us, and it does not matter what anyone else's journey looks like.  This is about our own connection and if someone experiences something different to you, that is absolutely how it should be.  The only focus here is you.

Ok, let's get started.

## Chapter Four

# I Feel Good
# (Raising your Vibration)

Mastering the art of feeling good without any guilt is not an easy task. It sounds so simple, doesn't it? But years of conditioning have made us feel that we must put others needs before our own. As Mothers/Wives/Partners/Employees there is always someone that wants something from us or a task that needs doing. This is not going to change for you overnight **but change it must**.

Why is this even relevant, let alone important?

Our emotional state has been supressed for decades and we have shut ourselves off from all the wonder and the magic because we have become obsessed with busying ourselves to the point of exhaustion. We have left ourselves absolutely no time to stop and just BE.

We are not giving ourselves the slightest chance to feel fulfilled and at peace and whilst you *could* communicate with your Angels from this heightened, chaotic state of stress and lack, you will get a much better experience and result if you clear out some of the crap beforehand. Similarly, the clearer the channel is for communication between you and your Angels, the more you will receive from them and the easier it will become.

And so, we begin our quest to find ways to make ourselves feel good and bring our awareness back to what is truly important. Before you start with all of the questions, this is a reminder to look at what I said in the last chapter (and hopefully now you will begin to understand why I said it)

If it feels good to you, keep doing it. If it doesn't then stop. Just because it works for one person, does not mean it will work for you.

Take meditation, for example. This ancient practice is used by millions of people around the world but I, personally, struggle to sit and clear my head for an extended period. The thoughts and distractions pop back in and it then becomes less about the calming breath and more about me fighting with my thoughts and telling myself that I am doing it wrong.

If it is a guided meditation where someone else is telling me what to do then I can relax into it more but even then, after about 15 minutes I get fidgety - and that is OK.

Meditation is a practice of connecting to yourself but so is journaling, so is getting out into nature, so I do those instead, because that is what works for me. You simply need to find what works for you and remember not to overcomplicate it. **Keep it simple**. You will know if it works for you because you will look forward to doing it, it won't feel like a chore, and you always feel better after you have done it.

I want you to think about all the activities that you enjoyed as a child. What are your happiest memories? What hobbies have you given up on due to other peoples' demands on your time? Remember, the aim is to *feel good* and reinforce that feeling so it grows until we crave it every day and it becomes just who we are.

It might take some time at first, especially if you are not used to putting yourself first, and you may feel guilty about taking half an hour to enjoy a bubble bath or going for a walk but stick with it. If you cannot commit to doing this simple thing for yourself, then the truth is that this is just not for you – except that it absolutely is! Love yourself enough to try it – it can be 10 minutes of playing a couple of your favourite songs that make you feel good. Do not tell me you do not have a spare 10 mins in your day!!

Let us address some of the questions that I know you want to ask.

- Have I got to do it every day?
- How long is it going to take?
- Where do I start?
- How do I know if I am doing it correctly?
- Am I going to hear voices?
- Do I have to do just one thing or multiple things?
- Do I have to get up early to do it before I go to work?
- What about the weekends? Can I take a day off?
- How will I know if I am making it up or if it is real?
- Will anything strange happen to me?
- Will I start seeing things?
- How soon will it work?

Blah, blah blah.

I am not going to address every question that you may have, because to be brutally honest, if you are asking anything resembling these questions, then you are completely missing the point.

This isn't about getting it done. This is about understanding YOU. This is about discovering the magic of a world which, up until now, you have not truly seen. This is about questioning a lifetime of other people's beliefs that you have taken on as your own. Do not underestimate just how flipping incredible this is – the decision alone to even consider this as a possibility for you is HUGE. The understanding will come to you in the most unexpected ways and the most seemingly insignificant word, picture or verse of a song may be given to you and the realisation that you experience could truly blow your mind – and you want to rush through it??

Ok, Louise, BREATHE.

Remember there are no rules. Remember to do what feels good to you. There is no should or should not. Like anything, the more you do something, the more familiar it will become, thereby making it more likely that you will continue to do it. At first it may feel clunky and uncomfortable as most things do the first time, we try them. I doubt very much that you will have done all that you need to do in just one month when there are decades of stories for you to clear out and understand.

It is totally ok to start and stop as you feel appropriate. We all have life to deal with and sometimes it is just not possible. The more you put into it, the more you will get out of it and the easier and clearer your communication will become.

If you are still unsure where to start, a (simple) gratitude practice will raise your vibration to a higher state and increase your awareness of what is really around you. You can list 5-10 things that you are grateful for every day, preferably in the morning, as it gets your day off to a great start, but the evening is fine too. The point is, if you like the idea that there may be more to life than what you have experienced so far, you have nothing to lose by giving this a go. You could even ask the Angels to help you (more on this to come)

This is *your* spiritual journey and reading this book has already moved you along your path. What you choose to do with the information is up to you. I, WE, really, really hope that you will continue to explore and learn and grow and build your own connections to the Angels and make your life more about ease and flow and less about running on that hamster wheel.

Once you become familiar with feeling good, you will be able to look at some of your past experiences with a different perception and change the way you feel about them. You will no longer think that you were stupid or insignificant because your life is starting to feel better and those things no longer have a place, as they resided in the negative vibrational life that you used to lead. There will, of course, be some bigger, more stubborn events that you continue to carry around, but we are all about celebrating progress, not about looking at what we haven't yet achieved.

It is going to take time so the sooner you get started, the sooner you will be able to feel good.

## Chapter Five

# Dear Darling (The Art of Journaling)

This is my go-to practice. This is important. Don't be a know it all and skip this chapter.

I want you to treat yourself to a lovely new journal or notebook - it doesn't need to be expensive, but the fresh, new energy that it holds will definitely help you to feel excited at trying something new, (even if you have journaled before this *is* new as you are coming from a different place, having set the intention for change earlier on. This will also signify to the Universe that you are serious about taking action on your dreams.

Then make some time for yourself. YOU HAVE THE TIME SO DON'T EVEN TRY TO MAKE EXCUSES.

Give yourself 15 minutes of uninterrupted, quiet time where you can sit and just BE. Think in your mind about what you would like in that moment - do not try and control it or force yourself to think of something you think that you should have. What do YOU want?
Open your journal and just let the words come. You can start it as a letter - Dear Diary, Dear Universe, Dear Angels, I would really like X, Y, Z and let all of the thoughts and feelings you have around it out and onto the paper.

This can be a desire for something in the future or support to help you right now. You will find that you will desire different things as you continue because your perceptions will change and what was once important to you may have fallen away and you may desire something new.

You might get given a word - if you do, write it down. You may see something in your mind's eye. You may get nothing at all and whatever you do or do not get is absolutely right for you.

It may take some time to understand what the relevance is of anything that comes to you, but trust and know that it will. You are building a connection that most people do not even know is available to them and you are opening yourself up to a new way of being – if they gave it all to us after the first journaling session, we would all run to the hills, screaming!! The important thing to remember here is that you have started. Feel excited about what is to come.

You don't always have to ask for a physical thing, and I am going to give you some examples of these as many people do not realise that this is possible. When people talk about manifesting, (getting stuff), it can often relate to a house, a car, a relationship, or money, and whilst all of these are completely valid, sometimes all we want is our day to go well, without any unnecessary drama.

Some examples to give you an idea.

❖ Resolving a tricky situation with a loved one calmly and lovingly.

❖ Feeling high vibe at work when you have an important meeting that would otherwise leave you feeling overwhelmed.

❖ The perfect parking space, right outside the shop you need to go to.

❖ No queues at your checkout when doing the weekly shop.

❖ An easy journey on your drive to a new destination.

❖ A restful and revitalising night's sleep before an important day.

- ❖ To find laughter throughout your day. (This is one of my faves).

- ❖ To gain clarity around a situation that is currently confusing.

- ❖ Asking for a sign if you are struggling with a decision (more on this to come).

- ❖ Inspiration for something you are working on or want to explore.

- ❖ Feeling calm.

- ❖ Gaining a loving perspective around something that has been troubling you.

- ❖ Letting go of negative experiences and emotions (cutting cords).

The list truly is endless.

By getting it out of your head and into the physical world onto paper, you have not only made space to be able to receive but you have increased your awareness around it and are therefore more likely to be open and aware when it comes along.

### "All that from just writing a few lines in a notebook?"

Yep. Like I keep telling you, it *is* easy, and you will soon discover that this will become a gorgeous habit for you. You will enjoy it so much you will want to do it every day. You will build *momentum* and the more you do it, the clearer it will become and the more will come back to you. Some days you may just want to write about how you are feeling - if you are struggling with a certain situation or you may just want to write a letter to a loved one who has passed to bring closure. You may just want to have a rant because you have had an argument with someone, and you are angry.

It does not matter what you write. It just matters that you **write**. I have never regretted getting my journal out and even if I don't know what to write, I will start with 'I don't know what to write today as I am feeling a bit lost' and the rest will come. It never fails.

Ok, I am sensing some resistance here.

Some of you are already overthinking about not knowing what to write and if it is the right thing to ask and what if nothing happens ….

If you approach any spiritual practice (raising your vibration) from this place of fear, you are going to make it extremely difficult for yourself.

I know it is easy for me to say, but you have to *trust* that this is going to work for you. Go back to the intention setting practice that we did and repeat it, or at least read it again and remind yourself of why you are doing this.

Respect the Angels enough to honour what they are saying because, quite frankly, they really cannot make it any easier for you.

It is vital that you fully understand this, as it applies to *everything* that you do from here on in. So, if you are rushing to find 15 mins before doing the school run and have one eye on the clock and the other on the pile of washing in the corner, you are not going to be successful. And what I mean by that is that you can ask but the chances of you receiving what you have asked for will be greatly reduced as your mind is on auto pilot.

The song on the radio that mentions the colour yellow that you asked about will be drowned out by you moaning to your friend how hard your life is.

The sign of a flamingo that you wanted to see has just driven past you on the side of a lorry but you were too busy scrolling on your phone whilst you waited for your kids.

Remember what I said about the orbs? They had always been there, but I had not been in the right *vibrational place* to see them. What I don't want to happen is that you half-arse it and then when you think you haven't received your answer, you give up and throw the book across the room!

So, anyway, what the heck does this have to do with Angels, I hear you all asking?

You are shifting and clearing out the day-to-day thoughts, unscrambling your busy mind and you are, ultimately, giving them *space* to reach you and they will, if you allow them to.

It is a bit like having a good old clear out of your drawers at home. You know the ones I am referring to - the ones that are full of junk- the stuff we keep just in case and every time you go to it you struggle to find what you are looking for even though you are sure it is in there. Once you clear out all of the unnecessary stuff the next time you go to that drawer you will instantly see that thing you have been looking for.

It is the same thing with our minds. We get so caught up in our day to day lives, worrying about hundreds of things all the time that we drown out so much of what is around us. We are so preoccupied with events that haven't even taken place yet and stressing about outcomes that we cannot control that we have lost sight of what is important and right in front of us.

You are supposed to have it easy. We want this for you, we want this for everyone. I cannot do this for you. If you truly desire change you have to do the work. You have to make a start.

What do you have to lose?

How bad do you want it?

I am still sensing some fear so, just for the record and to reassure you,

There is nothing to fear. A 10 ft Angel is not going to show up in your living room, just because you asked for a good night's sleep. Your Angels love you unconditionally and they will only ever guide you in a way that you can handle and trust and know that that it is them.

Some of you may never actually see them because that is too much for you and simply knowing that they are there is all the reassurance that you need.

So, what are you waiting for? At the very least you will have had 15 minutes to yourself and got some junk out of your head.

Do it, I dare you.

## Story Time

All the stories that I share are mine and completely true. They are not designed or included to prove anything - moreover just some recollections of situations that have occurred that seem illogical or impossible.

# The Hearing Aid

It was a cold, damp winter morning and I was on the early shift at work. It was 6:30 and no other staff had arrived when a car pulled into the car park and a little old man began to get out. I rushed out to him as our store wasn't due to open for hours but as I reached him, he was pacing up and down. He began to tell me he had come to the store the previous day and as he was loading his car, his hearing aid had fallen out. He thought it had dropped into the boot but when he got home, he discovered it wasn't there, so he came back in the hope of finding it on the ground. He was visibly upset and told me it was quite expensive, so I began to help him search, despite thinking to myself that we had no chance of finding it. He couldn't remember where he had parked so we had quite a task ahead of us.

"Hello, can I help?" A voice was behind me, and I spun around. This radiant woman was smiling at us. Stunned, I looked around the car park - there were no other cars. Where had she come from? I could not seem to speak so I turned back to the old man, but she had taken him by the arm across the car park and was listening intently to what he was saying and nodding and reassuring him that it would be ok. I felt unable to move as I watched her guide him to a spot nearby where she slowly bent down and picked something up off the ground.

"Here it is," she said. My jaw dropped to the floor. I ran over, absolutely dumbfounded. The man was thanking her over and over and as I walked him a few steps back to his car, I turned to thank her and there was no one there. She had vanished as suddenly as she had arrived.

## Chapter Six
# Rolling in the Deep

As I mentioned earlier, just by picking up this book, you have moved along your spiritual path. By getting your journal and writing in it has moved you yet again. The Angels see this. The Angels are excited about this - for you. For, they see you for all that you are - not the low vibrational thoughts that we flood our minds with every single day, but the powerful soul that you came on this earth to be.

The wheels are in motion, and you are moving forward every time you are present, every time you look up at the sky and breathe in the natural beauty that is all around you in that moment. You are connecting to the Universe and the Angels are drawing closer. Whilst all of this is true, you may not be aware of it for some time. It can be a challenge to believe and trust in something that you cannot see or feel (yet). But I need you to know this. I need you to take this into your heart and believe it with every fibre of your being.

**Every intention you set, every action you take, no matter how small or insignificant you perceive it to be, it really does matter and really does count. Nothing is a waste of time. If you try something and it doesn't work, you have learned a lesson. You cannot force this, and you cannot cut corners or rush it to suit your own timeline (trust me, I have tried).**

Like I have already touched on, I had almost 5 decades of stuff to work through and I truly believe that my time was supposed to be 2020 because I was furloughed for 9 months with nothing else to do nothing but 'the work'. It was ramped up immensely and the Angels came in early on to help me through it. That truly was divine timing at work. Some days I could not get out of bed – let alone hold down a job and there is no doubt in my mind it was always supposed to be this way.

Please do not let this put you off, though. I was not the only person that spent 2020 'waking up' in fact this was true for many and we are now shining our collective light out into the world to help more people discover who they truly are and we are here to make that experience easier for you as we have gone through it and know the pitfalls and what to look out for and to energetically accelerate you through the process.

Something that can be useful if you feel that you are 'stuck' or not moving forward, is to reflect on how far you have come already.

Another reason for keeping a journal is to look back and see how you were feeling, what you asked for and what guidance you received around it. Reflection is often overlooked but it gives such good insight into your progress, even just the words that you used at the very start will have changed, there will be a confidence in your latest entries and writing words like Angels and Universe will seem familiar, if not completely normal.

If it helps, think about it in terms of weight loss or joining the gym. You don't eat a salad for a day or walk on a treadmill for half an hour and completely transform your body (if only!). The same applies to doing this work and it is 'work'. Setting time aside when you could be watching TV or scrolling on social media to work on yourself and shift your energy to a place of higher vibration takes commitment, time, and a ton of self-love.

I cannot tell you how long it will take. You may not receive anything for a couple of weeks. You may receive something the first time you try it and not realise what it is.

Some days you may feel like you've cracked it and other days you may feel like you have gone back several steps. None of this is wrong.

Remember, we are doing this whilst navigating life. The pressures of the everyday routine are bound to affect us and it can feel like a waste of time or you are racing against the clock and have to make a choice to not do it that day. That is all ok. What we *don't* do, is punish ourselves or stop altogether. We are loving ourselves throughout this process because we want a better life for ourselves and those around us.

Remember to do what feels good. If you are stressing out about having no time, then leave it, but maybe you can listen to something uplifting in the car, walking to the shops, or whilst doing your chores. This is not a one-size-fits-all kind of deal, because we are all unique souls that require all sorts of different support and love for ourselves at different times. You do not have to do the same practice every day. You only have to feel into what you want to do and then do that with no judgement or pre conception that it is not what you *should* be doing. If it makes you feel good, it is right for you in that moment, and that is all we want. Being present, not over thinking and worrying about the next hour, the next week or something in the distant future is our goal. The here and now is all that matters. We must be open and adaptable to change and remind ourselves constantly why we are doing this.

*The Angel's Angle*

*The laws that govern the Universe are more powerful than we could ever truly understand. You are influencing these laws right now but there is much more work to be done here. Know that we are supporting you with this. It is not an ordinary thing you are doing by challenging all of what you know and choosing the way that you were all supposed to be and have been before you came here. You will experience huge shifts in your energy and some people may fall away as you naturally gravitate towards people (souls) that share your outlook on this incredible world. That is why it must be a gradual process – to prepare you for each stage of awakening and we will be right beside you, cheering you on. Keep going. You are doing so well.*

## Chapter Seven

# You're the Voice

I am hoping by this point, you are feeling a bit more open or curious as to what your life could look like.  I hope you are picking up on the possibilities that are around you.  This book is filled with activations which means that the words I have used are intentional and *intended* to spark something within you.  You may be feeling a tingling.  You may be feeling like you just want to get on with it.  You may be feeling absolutely nothing at all and, as always, that is what is completely right for you.

You may also feel like you want to know more and have turned to Google for the answers.  I did this too – so many times - and not once did it give me what I truly needed.

Asking a search engine what it means to see a white feather after you have journalled something personal to you is like asking a fish to ride a bicycle.

I know it's frustrating. I know you want all of the answers – *because that is how we have been programmed.*

Trust me (again) when I say you will thank me later and it will be worth it. The sense of achievement you will feel when you can master your vibration and connect in the moment for whatever you need is **so** powerful. I can give you the tools and *activate* curiosity within you but there is no shortcut. Unless, of course, you consider what I am about to share with you.

Bear in mind that the sole (soul) purpose of this book is to bring Angels into your everyday life. To make the process quick and easy and just something you do when you are brushing your teeth or in your car. This isn't about giving you more stuff to do.

Yes, your 15 minutes (or more) of journaling is a powerful tool and the more you commit to it, the more you will get from it, and if it feels good it can be a very easy way to receive guidance. I haven't asked anything else of you because I know that I am already asking a lot.

So, if I was now to describe to you a long, drawn-out process with candles and prayers and crystals and chanting whilst wearing a full-length robe, matching head dress and pointy slippers before declaring all sorts of complicated statements out loud, the chances are you would close this book right here and never open it again.

Of course, you can do all those things and more if you wish to - if it feels good to you - but you don't *have* to.

We are bringing something new, and you are one of the first to experience it. This is my life's work. This is what I came here to do, and I am finally sharing it with the world because spirituality does not need to be complicated.

Spirituality does not exist only for the elite or the devout. Spirituality is for *everyone.* We just need to shift our perspective on what it actually means to be spiritual because it is not an exclusive club. It is not limited to the rich and famous. You do not need a referral to join. There is no waiting list. (Yes, people are waking up more and more but in their own time which is perfect for them). You can access all of the magic with no premium subscription required. You can talk to your Angels today if you want to. Nothing is stopping you. Let go of all that you thought was true. Try it this way.

This is how I imagine the following conversation to go when I tell you how to do it.

**ME**:   JUST ASK THEM (The Angels).

**YOU**: WHAT?!! (Thinking…..)

**YOU**: That's It???

**ME**:   Yep.

**YOU**: Well, that can't be right, surely?

**ME**:   Why not?

**YOU**: Because it can't be that simple!

**ME**:   Why not?

**YOU**:  Because if it was everyone would be doing it!

**ME**: (Grinning like a Cheshire Cat)
## Why do you think I wrote the book???

SILENCE………Mic drop.

## Are you hearing me in the back??

Ok, so the next bombshell I am going to drop on you is how you ask. Wait for it….

**HOWEVER THE FUDGE YOU WANT**

Allow me to explain this 'crazy' notion.

Remember the rules? Just do what feels good. It applies to everything when it comes to your spiritual practices. I *know* that I am repeating myself, but it needs to be said numerous times. This is not learning in the traditional sense. This is not school, and I (we) will not score your work or tell you to do better or that you are doing it wrong.

BECAUSE YOU CANNOT DO IT WRONG!

Let me clarify this. Sometimes, we just feel the need to complicate our lives and make it so incredibly unnecessarily difficult. Why?

*Because that is what our parents and their parents before them did.*

*Because we love to focus on and talk about all our struggles.*

*Because we have been programmed to believe that life is hard, and sacrifice is good. Going without makes you virtuous. Having no money makes you a decent person. The rich are greedy, arrogant, and selfish. Nobody should have that much money. I bet they don't even know how to wash their own floors!* (This was one of my mother's favourites - even though it meant that they were *paying* someone else to do it for them)

## *BULLSHIT ALERT!!!*

It *can* be easy.
It *can* be magical.
It *can* be amazing.
You *can* talk to them.
You *can* hear them.
You *can* feel them.
You *can* see them.


You *can* live a fulfilled, joyful, wondrous life and have a conscious connection to your Angels which is as easy and effortless *as you want it to be.*

Now, of course everyone is different (thank goodness), and we all have our own communication styles because that is part of who we are. BUT it can and will work for you because you now know how to recognise what feels good to you and that same practice applies here and throughout your life.

### The Angels' Angle

*"We are knocking on your door, waiting for you to invite us in. We will adapt to your soul and the desires it holds for you. So, we are challenging you to just ASK for a little something – maybe not a physical thing – more like a FEELING, an OUTCOME, a CHANGE in perspective. What is the worst that could happen? That you think we haven't kept our part of the bargain? That we didn't deliver what you asked for? (LOL)*

Who knew Angels said LOL???

They are calling you in right now. They are laughing, smiling, and loving that these words are finally going out into the world because they want everyone to know this There is no need to complicate any of this. It is available and accessible to every single soul on this planet, and I am delivering this message right now because it is more needed now than ever before. The world is waking up at a rapid rate and people need to know that all the help they need is just one ask away.

## Story Time

This is a perfect example of all that we have covered in the previous chapter.

# The Text Message

When I talk about receiving in the moment, I really am not joking!

I had had a very bad night of broken sleep and had just fallen back to sleep when the alarm went off. I repeatedly hit the snooze button until it dawned on me that I was now very late for work. I pulled myself up and sat on the edge of my bed and looked at the clock in utter despair. There was no way I was getting to work on time this morning and I was not up for the conversations that would then have to take place as to why I was late and staying on to make the time up. Everything about that situation felt really ick and therefore out of alignment for how I wanted my day to go.

I closed my eyes and took a deep breath. "Angels, I need more time," I said out loud. My phone instantly beeped.

I opened my eyes. It was a message from a work colleague, telling me he was going to be at least half an hour late for work and as he had the keys to get in, I needed to stay at home until he got there! I laughed out loud, thanked the Angels, and got back into bed.

## Chapter Eight
# Sign of the Times (Signs)

This is amazing, by the way.

This is just all of the things. Not forcing, allowing, trusting, connecting – it is just *everything*.

So, this is a perfect example of a chapter that I did not know was going to be written, despite having had constant signs that it was on its way.

Music is such a powerful conduit for me to receive messages as it lifts my vibration, makes me feel good and therefore makes me more open to allowing and receiving. It is absolutely no coincidence that every one of these chapters is the title of a song. So, when I saw Harry Styles floating across the sky on my TV, despite not having asked him to, I did wonder what was going to come of it. He has been quite insistent, popping up in the middle of my You Tube music and as he is not someone I usually listen to (don't hate me), my curiosity was piqued.

This has happened numerous times before, but usually through artists that I enjoy watching, which makes more sense as I am more inclined to listen, so when this handsome devil kept showing up, I thought he is either after my body or I had better find out what they are trying to tell me.

I went for a walk, not intentionally to find out the guidance, but because my baby Granddaughter was teething, and I didn't know what else to do with her. We walked for over an hour and as soon as she fell asleep, I felt myself relax as we took a nice gentle stroll along the beach, and I stopped to take in the sunshine. I heard a voice that said, 'Look Up' and as I did a golden light moved across the sky towards the sun. An Angel was saying hello and I knew that I was exactly where I was supposed to be in that moment. I carried on my walk and as I huffed and puffed up the hill with the pram, sounding like I was taking my last breath, I got it.

'LOUISE, TELL THEM ABOUT THE SIGNS. THEY WANT TO KNOW ABOUT SIGNS!!!'

Me: 'OHHHHH….., Ok! Why didn't you just tell me that??

And that, Ladies and Gentlemen, is what we are now going to get into. Before we do that though, there is something I need to get off my chest.
 There does seem to be somewhat of a blasé attitude around receiving or seeing Angel Signs. White feathers, silver coins and rainbows are very popular signs that people ask for, but when they are shown them, instead of feeling inspired and grateful, they question what they have seen and often ask for another sign to confirm that this was in fact THE sign.

**DO NOT DO THIS.**

**EVER.**

I cannot express how completely disrespectful I find this! To dismiss out of hand a personal, spiritual sign, that has been delivered to you directly from the universe in response to your desires, has absolutely no place in the world. You are being given exactly what you asked for so please show it the appropriate level of respect and gratitude if you want more to follow. Ok, rant over.

As you move through your journey, your signs will evolve alongside you and the feathers that I see daily are more of a hello message than an answer to a specific question. A reminder that wherever I go, they are with me and that never fails to make me smile.

What is not often talked about, though, is the magnitude of the signs that are available to you if you do not close yourself off to the idea that anything is possible.

This photo was taken on 16 February 2021 at 19:45, minutes before I was going to do my very first You Tube video and open my channel to the public. It was something I had wanted to do for so long and this was a huge confirmation for me that I should go ahead and make a start. The Angels were showing me that they were all with me, supporting me and loving me as always. Of course, they are not always so grand, but I wanted you to know that they absolutely can be.

June 2020 – when things just started getting juicy! I was questioning everything and wanting to run away and hide. I felt close to giving up because it felt too overwhelming to keep going back to that place of pain and dealing with the past. Then, I looked up and saw my team of Angels dancing in the sky, showing me that they were there.

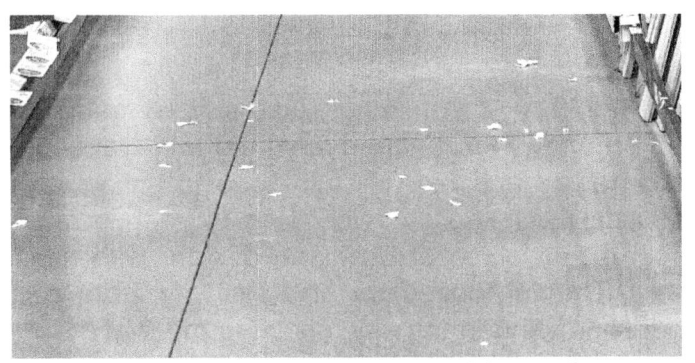

The very first time I received guidance for someone else and activated her connection to her Angels, I was at work and after I had shared the guidance with her, I looked down to see all these bright white feathers around my feet.

I guess the point that I am wanting to make here is that your signs are unique to you and just because I see Angels in the clouds all the time, you may see something different- maybe an animal, or a heart, or anything that you can relate you.  But, it doesn't stop there because you can receive signs from all sorts of places and I do not want to you to shut yourself off from all of the possibilities.  I want you to let go of the more traditional thought of what a sign must look like and be open and excited for something new, because the more unexpected the sign is, the more powerful the message is for you and the stronger your connection will become.

      I don't want to limit your expectations, but I am going to give you a few examples of signs/guidance/confirmation that I have received.

- ❖ A song on the radio that is saying the exact words I need to hear and sends shivers down my spine.

- ❖ A TV advert that I may have seen countless times before but in that moment gives me an answer.

- ❖ Overhearing a conversation of two strangers that are talking about the very thing that has been on my mind.

- ❖ Words on the side of a lorry, or a logo

- ❖ Number plates that remind me that all is well and that I am on the right path.

- ❖ A product popping up on my social media scroll that is the exact item that I have been looking for and its 50% off

- ❖ A spiritual mentor or coach going live to talk about the exact subject that I needed clarity on.

- ❖ Angels showing up on my TV screen to remind me that they are always with me which always leads to the answer I have been seeking.

I hope that this shows you that there are countless ways to receive a sign and, as with everything else, this will be unique to you, and you will find what your go-to method is as your connection builds.

If I am not going for a walk to find out the answer, which may then show up in any of the ways I have listed, I will put on the TV, ask out loud for what it is I need to hear and wait to see who shows up.  It is that easy and that flipping magical, because I have done the work and I completely trust and know that the answer will come at the perfect time.  It always does

## Story Time

# The Car

My Husband decided it was time for a change of car, and this has historically always been a bit of a stressful experience, mainly because the man just cannot make a decision, but this time it was an absolute joy.

We went to test drive a very nice-looking car that had all the bells and whistles on that he wanted. I could see in his face that he wanted it, but I pretended not to notice. As soon as we sat inside it, I said 'This is not your car.' I could not tell him why other than it just did not *feel* right. He didn't say anything.

He drove it for about 15 minutes, and I could see how much he was enjoying it, so I once again reminded him that that it wasn't the one. As we returned to the dealership, he began reversing it into its space when he stopped abruptly. The reversing sensors were not working. I got out and stood in front of the car as he inched forward. The parking sensors weren't working either.

I said nothing. After a long conversation with the salesperson, it transpired there were other works that had not been done and it was all getting a bit complicated so I cut the conversation short and said we would think about it, knowing full well that we were never coming back.

Later that evening, another car popped up. As soon as I saw the first picture and read the blurb from the dealer, I told him 'This is your car.' He didn't reply (I get that a lot). I then asked what is the number plate? It feels important for some reason. He read it out, but it was nothing special, yet I still had the nagging feeling that I needed to know.

So, we went to see it. He fell in love with it, and I fell in love with the Great Dane that belonged to the owner and the car is now sitting on our drive.

This morning he said, 'Oh, the car previously had a private number plate.' Cue goosebumps. 'Go on, I said, although I already knew. 'S777_ _ _'

The tingles were running up and down my body at a crazy rate and then I got it. That was the *confirmation* that this was the right car!

Yet another example of how Angels can help you in your everyday life if you trust what feels good to you.

### Chapter Nine

# Let it Go.

You are all singing it in your head, aren't you?

This step, or next part of the process is often branded or labelled as tough or difficult or the most challenging and I am here to shout from the rooftops that it simply isn't true. In fact, it couldn't be further from the truth.

Why? Because you have done all that you need to do. You have tuned into what you want, and you have asked. It is irrelevant how you did this and what you asked for. So, now what? Let me first tell you what you *don't* do.

- ❖ You don't sit around impatiently, checking your phone to see if £10,000 has landed in your bank account.

- ❖ You don't become obsessed with how the answers will come.

- ❖ You don't try and control the outcome - e.g., if you asked for a sign of a flamingo, don't start searching for flamingo pics online or on your phone.

- ❖ You don't begin questioning and not trusting after 5 minutes because nothing has seemingly changed in your reality.

Just because you cannot see it, does not mean that nothing is happening.

The only thing that is required is for you to go about your day, content in the knowledge that the answers will come.  They always do, but in order to receive them you need to keep up your end of the bargain, which is keeping your vibration high, so you are in alignment to your desires. If you have any free time, spend it intentionally doing something you enjoy and that relaxes you and *makes you feel good* (remember the rules?)  Make it easy for them to talk to you or show you or give you the feelings of what you have been asking for.  I often get guidance when I am cooking because I am focused on the task at hand, I am relaxed and looking forward to eating the meal that I am preparing.

If you struggle with this part of the process, the easiest thing to do is to keep your desires more general and much less specific. For example, avoid putting dates on your manifestations if it makes you feel panicky as the date draws nearer. If you are asking for an outcome, say for a job interview, try wording it a different way and ask for either this job or something better that is for my greatest good. The whole point is to feel good about your desires, not stressed out and worried when they are going to show up. And then, for example, later that day, you may see an advert for a completely different job that you had never thought of, and it feels so good to you that you apply, and it could be the job of your dreams! Can you see that by shutting yourself off, you are limiting your possibilities.

At the risk of repeating myself (I may just copy and paste this at the bottom of every page) It is *that* simple. There is not forcing, no pushing or stressing - nothing about this is rushed or chaotic. Remember, you are unlearning all that you once thought was your life, so accepting that it does get to be this easy for you may seem a step too far for you right now. But imagine, for just a moment, what I am telling you is true and available to you in every moment of every day. Why wouldn't you want a piece of the action?

## Chapter Ten

# How Will I Know?

We have already talked about signs, but we are going there again.

Let us imagine the scene… You have followed the steps and asked for a sign and, to the best of your ability have tried to focus on enjoying your day. Your sign is a rainbow and by lunchtime it hasn't shown up, so you decide to go for a drive to take your mind off it.

After a few minutes, you pull into a supermarket car park and the car in front has a bumper sticker with a rainbow on it.

You stare at it for a few seconds and rather than cheering, acknowledging, celebrating, and thanking the Angels for the sign, you begin a very detailed list in your head of all the logical reasons that this is not your sign.

Such as, it's not a real rainbow so it doesn't count (FYI it totally counts).

It is just a coincidence that you saw it as you were not planning to go to the supermarket today, so what would have happened if you hadn't gone? (FYI it was absolutely no coincidence)

It was really small - I was expecting it to be so much bigger so it was obvious it was my sign. Maybe it is someone else's sign - maybe they asked to see a small rainbow (even though you didn't actually specify) Yes, this is definitely not my rainbow. I will ask *again*; can I have a sign that the rainbow was in fact my actual sign or has my actual sign not even showed up yet???

The Angels are chuckling right now because this happens so much, and it is perfectly understandable, and they want you to know that there is nothing but love and support here for you and you will succeed. (By the way, you won't be getting another sign).

Now, let us imagine a different scene. This is one of my first experiences of intentionally asking for a sign.

I had joined a free challenge on Facebook about manifesting and this was the first task.

I was curious but not totally sure that it could happen for me. So, we had 24 hours for the sign to appear and soon people began posting in the group about their signs showing up.

I had asked for a windmill - it was the first thing that came into my head, so I went with it. (Intuition right there, even though I didn't know it).

I honestly gave it very little thought as I wasn't sure I believed in it, (sorry, team), but I had until the following evening for it to show up.

On a side note, putting time frames on things is not something that I normally do as it makes me feel restricted and trapped in a box, but like I said this was a group challenge and they were the parameters.

So, the evening rolled on and I was feeling unsettled. The TV was annoying me, and I felt too fidgety to read or get my journal out. I know, I said to myself, I'll have a few minutes playing my game.

Now this game is a very simple farming type situation that I have downloaded onto my phone, and it is great for distracting me for a few minutes and has quickly become one of my go-to tools when I want to quickly shift how I am feeling because I become focused on what I am doing that everything that was bothering me in that moment just simply fades away.

So, I open my phone, grateful for the distraction and load the game.

I look at the screen and cannot believe my eyes, for there, on my little virtual farm, was a WINDMIL!

I must have seen it 100 times before, but I never knew it was there. I was covered in goosebumps, and I just burst out laughing and gave the Angels a round of applause. It did not occur to me for a second to question it. I felt the nudge to go on the game and that was why.

Can you see the difference?

***I want you to go and create a JOY list.***

***Recognise what you enjoy spending time doing and write it down.***

*** Think of it as a toolbox that you can go to quickly and easily to get you aligned to that place of utter surrender.***

*** Only put things on the list if you truly enjoy doing them, not because you think that is what you should be doing.***

*** If you don't enjoy going for walks, then don't flipping go! If you are not a fan of a bubble bath, (I much prefer a shower) then don't put it on your list.***

***You might want to go for a run (my idea of a nightmare) or do some gardening.***
***Remember, there are only three rules – keep it simple, do what feels good to you and always show gratitude.***

I am feeling like you want a list so here are a few of mine but please don't do any of them if they don't feel aligned to you.

- ❖ Watching comedy shows

- ❖ Watching outtakes of comedy shows

- ❖ Kitchen disco with the music cranked up.

- ❖ Putting lovely backgrounds on my TV like a log cabin with a crackling fire and getting my journal out

- ❖ Napping with no guilt!  **Read that one again.**

- ❖ Cooking delicious, nutritious food that my soul desires

- ❖ Sunshine

- ❖ Watching classic black and white movies like Alfred Hitchcock

- ❖ Decluttering - whether it be digital as in apps, online groups, and people or physically in my home.  This is always a good idea because it shifts stagnant *energy* and creates space for new things to come to you.

## Story Time

# The Hotel Room

September 2022 and we were off on our first holiday abroad since 2018 and I was so excited. I had done a lot of intention setting for the journey to be an easy and effortless experience and it was – until we got to the hotel.

We stood in the queue whilst the receptionist began the painstaking process of booking in the people ahead of us, each time it took longer, and the queue was now out of the door.

A member of staff had phoned in sick, and she was on her own. I tried to feel sympathy, but it was a struggle.

I could feel myself getting more and more worked up. This was not supposed to be happening.

We had been up since the early hours, it was hot, I was tired, and I just wanted to get into our room. Then the receptionist announced that the rooms would not be ready for at least another three hours, but we were quite welcome to sit at the bar and wait.

I could feel Michael's hand digging into my back, which was his way of telling me to keep quiet. I hate to think what my face looked like at that moment because it must have been contorted all out of shape as I struggled to keep the words in. I looked down at the floor and took a couple of breaths to calm myself down. Then I said in my mind

'ANGELS, PLEASE DO SOMETHING!' We were next up. The receptionist repeated all of the information that we had now heard for the fourth time, and she began to say that our room wasn't ready but did a double take as she looked at her clipboard. 'Oh, your room is ready!' She looked very puzzled as I said a silent thank you. As we got to the room this is what I saw and, once again, I laughed out loud.

## Chapter Eleven

# All I Ask (Angel Cards)

I thought this was an important subject to include, not only because they have been a huge part of my understanding and receiving, but because they are a tangible tool that you can use to get you started which requires very little preparation or thought. Before we go any further, though, I have completed two paid courses to delve deeper into this subject and gain a certification, but that absolutely does not mean that you need to. The truth is you don't actually *need* cards at all, if you could find a way to completely trust your guidance, but that takes time, and a deck of cards can help you move forward with your connection in an easy, effortless and enjoyable way.

As with everything else, I am not going to tell you that you should or shouldn't have cards. I am not going to tell you which cards to buy. Once again, it is how it *feels* to you. I was strongly drawn to the deck that I use every day. Some people have multiple decks. Some people will carry out complex spreads of cards and spend a lot of time doing so. Others, like me, may just pull one card in the morning after asking a specific question. There are countless ways that you can utilise them and if it feels like something you would like to explore, there is a wealth of knowledge out there, but remember, just because someone is doing it a certain way, does not mean that you must. Some days, if I have more time, I may do a 3,6, or 9 card spread, particularly if it is the start of the month or I have a situation that I need answers to. I do it when I feel the nudge.

Just a few more points on this before we move on as I don't want this to become a tutorial on how to use them! Most decks come with a guidebook that you will give you an idea around what the message is, and it is absolutely ok to refer to that in the beginning, but I would also say, just sit with the answer for a minute and see how that truly relates to you and the question you have asked.

The more you do this, the more you will be able to translate the messages for yourself. I also need you to remember, that just because you pulled a card yesterday and it meant one thing, it can mean something completely different the next time that you pull it. This is all about your *energy* in the moment that you are asking and what it is that you are asking for.

I am going to give you an example as I feel you need further clarity to grasp this.

| TAKE CHARGE AND ACTION |
|---|

You may pull this card after asking 'What do I need to do today in order to move forward in my business?'

When you feel into the answer, it might be that you have been procrastinating around a certain area of your business and putting it off. You may be holding fear around being seen or putting your offering out into the world. You may even experience a mild physical reaction to this in your body, such as a tightness in your chest or a dry throat and these are all indications that you are understanding how this message relates to you.

So, in this instance, the guidance would be more around addressing those feelings and releasing the fear you have around them rather than actually taking what you may perceive as physical action like going live to talk about a special offer.

You may also pull this card when you are feeling 'stuck' and maybe a little uninspired or unmotivated or have lost your momentum. *Then* this card could mean a direct instruction for you to do something about it, because that is the only way for you to shift your energy and therefore begin to build the momentum once again.

Is this making sense? I am really trying to simplify this and show you that the only way to truly understand the answer, is to go within as there will be a part of you, and you will know it, that it is relevant to, whether you want to hear it or not! The final point I want to highlight here is this.

THE FIRST CARD IS ALWAYS THE RIGHT CARD FOR YOU.

Don't be tempted to put it back and try again. Often, the same card will come out anyway!

I really hope this chapter has been useful. Not all of you will want to try this, but if you do, remember to have fun with it, be light and expectant that what you need will come through and if you don't get an answer straight away, just let it go and it will be shown to you at some point throughout the day when you have loosened your grip on it.

## Chapter Twelve

# Fighter

I would like to think that by now you have picked up on how I like to keep things real with you. What is the point otherwise? If I tell you this is just soooo easy and you have to do nothing to connect to Angels, that it will just happen magically, you may *like* the idea initially until you very quickly realise that it doesn't actually work.

So, with that in mind, let me tell you about last night. I had spent most of the day working on the book and feeling pretty good about it. I was, however, feeling a sense of impatience growing inside of me as I really wanted it finished. Not for any other reason than I wanted it out in the world and to be able to talk about it and actually get things moving for so many of you. I have thoroughly enjoyed this writing process and I am, quite frankly, blown away by the guidance that has come through. But I still wanted it done. There were a couple of chapters that I cannot seem to complete, and they have been that way since I started.

I read through them for the umpteenth time and despite asking for more, I got a big fat zero.

I went for a walk and the Angels came with me. I took deep breaths and looked to the sky for answers. Nothing. I came back home and got out my journal (I do all the things that I talk about) and began to write but the agitation and frustration was growing inside of me, so I quickly closed it and went to cook dinner, knowing that I needed to leave it for a while. I soon became distracted with and felt much more relaxed about it, convinced that I would soon receive *something* so I could get moving again.

The evening rolled along, and I had put the TV on to keep my mind from solely focusing on the book, or rather the lack of it but it was still niggling.

I could feel it rising in my chest which was starting to feel tight. I tried to force ideas to finish the chapters which were weak at best. My mind was beginning to spin, and I could feel myself getting angry. I began to shout out loud.

**'WHY WON'T YOU JUST TELL ME WHAT I NEED TO KNOW?!!'**

**'WHY HAVE I GOT TO HAVE A TIGHT CHEST AND FEEL MAD WITH YOU? WHY ARE YOU MAKING THIS SO DIFFICULT FOR ME? WHY CAN'T I JUST FINISH THE F*****G BOOK??!!!'**

I grabbed my journal, and this is what happened.

ME: I hate you so much right now.

I took a deep breath. I didn't feel bad for writing that because in that moment I was overwhelmed with that feeling.

I began to write, extremely fast, unaware of the words.

MESSAGE: *'Despite everything it is not all rainbows and butterflies. Of course, we get frustrated when we want to know more, and we don't know how. Your knee jerk reaction is to lash out when you just need to take a minute to understand.'*

I read it back. Got covered in goosebumps. I understood.

I was supposed to go through that so I could write a chapter about it so that you all understood that sometimes it is not always easy. Sometimes you will doubt, and you will question and that is all part of building your connection. They do not judge, they do not mind, for they know the lesson that you will learn once you have been through it and are out the other side.

I couldn't finish the book yet because this chapter hadn't been written. It made complete sense.

This is such an incredible example of everything I have talked about. My resistance, my trying to force and control an outcome and my complete surrender (albeit by shouting) and allowing it to come through. I feel very blessed right now to have been able to share that.

## Chapter Thirteen

# No Matter What

We are often way too hard on ourselves and spend a lot of time just focusing on our flaws. We compare ourselves to what we perceive to be perfection in others and inevitably come up short. We actively seek out our shortcomings and failures so we can play them over and over in our minds as a way to constantly remind ourselves of how crap we are. Mental health, anxiety, and depression all stem from this place, and it is no coincidence that it is soaring right now. It is almost like an addiction - this place we go to - it is familiar - we know it and, paradoxically, it makes us feel safe because it is where we have lived our whole life. Isn't that just completely ludicrous? How does that make you feel after reading that? It makes no sense and yet makes complete sense. The Angels are wanting you to know now that this is not how they see you - not even remotely close. You can start a new diet on Monday and eat a packet of biscuits on Tuesday and they will love you anyway.

You can plan to get up early at the weekend and workout, but instead spend it on the sofa, watching Christmas movies and they will not point a finger or shake their head. You could be late for work, forget to do the shopping, run out of petrol, get annoyed about something trivial, lose your handbag, call in sick at work when you're not - whatever it is, whatever you do that causes that spiral of thoughts and feelings inside of you, just know that the Angels love you, NO MATTER WHAT.

Why is this important? Because we don't want you to give up. We don't want your current thoughts to get in the way and stop you from moving forward because the more you do this, the more you will release those thoughts and the easier it will become. Yes, right now, that may seem unlikely or even impossible, but this message is coming through loud and clear for you to understand. If you cannot see or feel any love for yourself right now, please please remember this. The Angels see all that you are doing and are applauding every single hurdle and obstacle that you have overcome. They know what is coming next for you and are urging you to dig deep and trust that you can do this. Your resolve is so much stronger than you know, and you *will* overcome this and begin to feel love for everything, including yourself.

So, when it feels impossible and you are overwhelmed and full of frustration, remember in that moment that you have an entire TEAM cheering you on and supporting you. No, it probably *won't* feel like it, but the more you draw on that, accept that and trust that, the more you will feel it and the more it will spur you on. Please don't give up. This will be your biggest achievement to date and the feelings you will get will be like nothing you have ever experienced before.

## STORY TIME

# The Missing Cards

Early March 2021 and I had been receiving guidance on doing Angel card readings for some time. I had completed a course and become certified (which wasn't at all necessary by the way). I purchased my first deck of cards from a beautiful soul who is in my online world. I was excited but once I had received them, I started to question whether I could do this.

Who would want to pay me for a reading when there are already so many gifted and talented people out there doing it. The voice in my head was very convincing and I told myself I would just use the cards for myself - to help me when I needed it. I had been kidding myself this whole time thinking I could ever make a go of it.

So, when I went to bed that night, I had resigned myself to this reality and it felt heavy on my heart but I couldn't argue with the powerful evidence my subconscious mind played over and over to me.

It was for the best and at least this way, I was safe and wouldn't have to face the inevitable failure that would follow if I tried. (This makes me feel so sad to write this now).

The next morning, I went to put the cards away as I didn't want to look at them for a while, but they weren't there. I stood, staring at my sofa where I had spread them all out the night before and it was bare, not a card to be seen anywhere. I just stood there, as if my feet were glued to the floor, trying to make sense of it. I had definitely left them right there so where on earth had they gone? I began searching frantically. Under the sofa, behind the sofa, around the sofa. Nothing. As I turned around, the card box was laying on the coffee table. I picked it up and four cards fell out.

- Be inspired and shine your light. The world is in need of your gifts, your creativity and your love. Do not hide in the shadows for you bare a bright light and your heart and soul glow so beautifully.

- Follow the divine guidance of your inner voice. Trust your intuition, for your heart and soul know the truth. Believe it, have faith.

- Be the change. Be the torch. Be the light. Lead the way. For your strength and love is guiding those who need it the most.

- You are beautiful, you are gifted, you are a divine spiritual being. Call on the me for guidance and support in growing and channelling your gifts and I will guide you every step of the way.

Eight days later, I saw a post on social media about sharing a picture of yourself and telling people a little bit about you. Back then, the very thought of this made me feel physically sick. I still had a lot of self-love work to do but I felt so strongly that I needed to do it. My hands were shaking but I did it. I told Facebook who I truly was and in that second, I heard 'Look under the sofa,'

You know what I am going to say next.

Yep, there were the cards, in the place I had looked at least 20 times. I had trusted the pull to post my pic and be seen and the Angels gave them back to me.

It was such a powerful message that I was infact ready to share who I truly was with the world.

## Chapter Fourteen

# Living on a Prayer

So, now what?

It is time for you to choose the way you want your life to look from today, going forward.

Wait, what, that's it?  No more practices, rituals, workbooks, courses, webinars, masterclasses, guided meditations, or journaling prompts for me to complete??

Don't we just love to over complicate our lives and make things difficult?  Of course, there is always inner work to do as we grow and evolve but right here, right now, you have all that you need to build a connection with your Angels.

The aim of this book was always to inspire you enough to get curious and try it for yourself. It is like any relationship that you have - it needs to build and grow and that takes time, energy, trust, and buckets of love. I can help you with it and this book will most definitely help you with it, but, ultimately, it is down to you.

You may want (in fact, we are encouraging you to), go back to the start and read it again. One of the reasons that this is a short, concise book with zero fluff is so you can easily refer back to it whenever you need to.

Set the intention in your mind that you want to grow your connection to your Angels. Grab your journal and write what this would look like for you. What do you want help with right now. How would you like to receive the guidance. What feels good to you about the process? Be grateful and thankful for what you will receive. Go back to any part that you feel you need further clarity on and just go for it. Follow the process just ask your Angels. You will not be disappointed.

*The Angels Angle*

*This is not so much a process as a state of BEING, for when you are open, we can guide you easily and effortlessly. This is not a job to get done, rather a total energetic shift of yourself and your vibration. Your soul is urging you to make this shift now so we can further support you in this wondrous life that is about to unfold for you.*

## Chapter Fifteen

# Lean on Me

So, it is time for you to step out into the big wide world and discover all of the magic for yourself. If that feels way too scary for you right now, if you feel like you need your hand holding for a bit longer, I would love to help you.

I offer bespoke Activating Angels Sessions that are tailored to meet you at wherever you are in your spiritual journey.

The sessions are based upon the principles in this book and are designed to either give you a head start or accelerate you to the next level of your connection and understanding.

These are a completely new service that I am offering which are specific to all that I have covered in here.

If you feel like this is something you might even be a bit curious about, please reach out to me and we can have a chat about what you need for you right now. The whole intention behind this work that I do is to activate your connection and help you move forward more quickly.

I would also love to hear your feedback after reading the book and any breakthroughs or shifts you have experienced. I know that this book is going to create change for so many and it would mean the world to me if any of you feel like sharing it with me.

Email: Angelslaughterandlove@gmail.com

Check out my social media links for more insight.

Instagram:
http://www.instagram.com/angels_laughterandlove

You Tube:
https://youtube.com/@Angelslaughterandlove

Just one more thing. I cannot do the work for you. I can empower you and motivate you. I can give you specific guidance on your next steps and I can highlight what is going on for you with your self-talk/self-love, but the rest is up to you. I say this with utter love, because you have to go through the process to gain your own understanding and perspective that is relevant to you and for you.

If this is the end of our journey together, at least for now, know that I will be cheering you on and rooting for you every step of the way and I truly hope and desire that you can find a beautiful connection with your amazing Angelic Team so you can experience magic and wonder in your own life.

I am so grateful to you for trusting me enough to read this book, because I am so incredibly proud and honoured to have been able to bring it to you.

There have been so many amazing coaches, mentors and teachers that have got me to where I am right now, whether I worked with them directly or not. They have helped me more than they could ever know and have expedited my journey and created a ripple effect as I am now bringing my own take on this out to the world. They show up every day, inspiring and motivating thousands of women, mostly for free, because they understand the importance of the change that is taking place in the world right now.

We need you and all that you are, to stand up as we rise together to bring more love into the world and a life for everyone that brings peace and joy. By just talking about this to your nearest and dearest, you are making a difference. By reading this book, you are making a difference. It does not need to be huge because you are making an impact every time you choose YOU and what feels good for YOU. Don't ever stop.

I have so much love for you all.

Louise
xxxx

Printed in Great Britain
by Amazon